Wolf Secret

Written by Lee Wang

Illustrated by Meredith Thomas

Flying Start
to Literacy®

Contents

Chapter 1
Victor's special job

Victor came rushing in the door after school.

"Is it time to feed the wolf cubs already?" asked his mother.

"It is," said Victor, as he rushed to the fridge to grab the pieces of elk meat that the wolves ate.

"Don't forget to stay well clear of the wolves when you feed them," said his mother. "We don't want them to pick up your scent and get used to your smells."

"I know," said Victor.

"The cubs are nearly old enough to go back to the forest where they need to survive by themselves," said his mum. "If these wolves are to fend for themselves they must not see humans as friends. They are wild animals. They need to stay away from people and hunt for their own food."

"Okay, but you don't need to worry, Mum," yelled Victor, as he bolted out the door and ran off to the nearby Wolf Refuge Centre.

Feeding the wolves was Victor's job. His parents worked at the Wolf Refuge Centre. They let him feed the five orphaned cubs that the Wolf Refuge Centre had been looking after ever since their mother had been killed by a falling tree.

Victor loved the thrill of being so close to wild and dangerous animals. He loved the sound of the wolves howling. It was exciting and scary all at the same time.

Victor's mother quickly left the house to catch up with him. She got to the wolf enclosure just as Victor stepped up to the fence. Victor placed the meat in the slot so it would slide down into the wolves' enclosure. He then quickly stepped back from the electric fence as his mum watched closely. The cubs began to sniff the air.

"Now, Victor, come back from that fence," whispered his mum. "They must not pick up our scent and get used to our smells."

"I know," said Victor.

Victor watched as the cubs sniffed the air, smelling to find the food. They ran to the meat and ate greedily until their stomachs looked like hard, round balloons.

Chapter 2
Watching the cubs

Victor loved to watch the young wolves and he had secretly given each cub a name. Lupa was his favourite.

She is so cute with her black face and white muzzle, thought Victor. I would love to pat her and play with her. I would love to be part of her family and to run and hunt with them, to belong to their pack.

But he knew this was wrong, so he stood back and watched closely.

Victor's mother then whispered, "I had better go home. Come in soon for dinner."

As Victor watched, he knew what would happen next. After the cubs had finished their meal, they would howl with pleasure. Lupa would always start. Victor listened and counted how many seconds each howl lasted.

1 ... 2 ... 3 ... 4 ... 5.
Then she howled again and waited for another wolf cub to return her call.

Lupa crouched down and wagged her tail before leaping on the other wolves. Victor smiled at the way they held their faces as they snarled and growled at each other while they played. Then they sat on their hind legs and sniffed the air. They knew there were strange smells not far away.

The wolf cubs came closer and looked at Victor. They looked at him as if they knew him. Victor's heart was pounding. He wanted to reach out and touch them.

But he stopped. He remembered what his mother had said. He could hear her calling in the distance. He left the wolf cubs and ran inside.

Over dinner, Victor's father said, "It is early spring. Our five cubs are now about ten months old and growing quickly. It's time for them to be returned to the wild. There will be young elk now for them to hunt and eat. I have called the ranger and he will come for them tomorrow."

Victor tried to hold back his tears. He had always known that one day the wolf cubs would have to go back to the wild, but he had hoped that the day would never come.

His father put his arm around him and said gently, "Tomorrow we will go to Yellowstone National Park to see them released. Then we can go for a walk to see the other young animals in the park."

Chapter 3
A sad parting

The next day Victor watched as the ranger loaded the wolf cubs into the back of his van. Then Dad and Victor followed them to Yellowstone National Park.

Lots of people had come to see the wolves being released in Yellowstone National Park. Some people were protesting. They didn't want the wolves released in the park because they thought the wolves were dangerous.

Victor hoped the cubs would not be too frightened by all the noise.

As soon as the cubs were let out of their cage, they all ran off into the forest. Victor closed his eyes and pictured their faces, especially Lupa's white muzzle.

He remembered her howls –

1 ... 2 ... 3 ... 4 ... 5.

Victor's father said, "The ranger is taking a group through the park. Why don't we go too? We might see the wolf cubs later in the day."

As Victor and his dad headed off down the track with the group, snow began to fall lightly. Victor couldn't stop thinking about Lupa and the other cubs.

Would they be okay?
Would they find food?
Would they miss him like he was already missing them?

The group moved on. Victor stopped to listen for the wolves' howls. He waited and listened, but there was nothing.

"Victor, keep up," said his dad.

"Be there in a second," yelled Victor.

Maybe if I look closely, I'll see their tracks, thought Victor.

As Victor wandered around looking for wolf tracks, a thick fog came down. When he looked up, he couldn't see his father or the other people in the group. It was getting dark and cold, and he couldn't see the track.

Victor ran in several directions trying to find the track. He knew that this weather was dangerous. It would get colder and colder, and if he had to stay out overnight, the air would become so cold it could kill him.

Then Victor saw some shadows in the distance. Was it his dad and the group? He couldn't see for sure. Should he call out?

Suddenly he was overcome with fear. What if it was a bear? Or a pack of wild wolves? What would he do?

Victor heard a low snarl from behind a tree. Then another. And another.
Could it be a bear?

Then the fog cleared, just a little, and Victor caught a glimpse of a white muzzle with a patch of black.

It was Lupa!

Chapter 4
A dangerous encounter

Lupa's teeth were bared and a low rumbling growl escaped her mouth.

She really is a wild animal, thought Victor. He backed away, but there was nowhere to go.

Then Lupa did something that Victor did not expect. She raised her head and began to howl.

1 ... 2 ... 3 ... 4 ... 5.

And again –

1 ... 2 ... 3 ... 4 ... 5.

And again –

1 ... 2 ... 3 ... 4 ... 5.

All the wolves in her pack returned her howl.

Victor shivered in fear. He didn't know what to do. Should he run? Should he talk to the wolf cubs? Would they remember his voice?

The wolves sniffed the air. Were they looking for food?

Just then, Victor heard his father call out, "Quick, over there."

At the sound of his father's shout, the pack of wolves quickly slipped away into the fog.

Victor's father ran up to him, dropped to his knees and hugged Victor tightly.

"I have been looking everywhere for you," said his dad, gasping for air. "When I heard that wolf, I was frightened that the pack had attacked you. I wonder how they found you?"

As Victor and his dad were hurrying to join the rest of their group, Victor's father said, "I am puzzled why the wolves howled that way near you. They don't usually do that."

Victor looked back over his shoulder, but the fog now formed a thick blanket over the trees. They howled that way because I am part of their pack, he thought. They looked after me. Wolves in a pack look after each other. That is what they do.

A note from the author

I have a special love of wild animals and like to visit places where I can observe wild animals behaving with freedom in their own wild homes. I always have good feelings about wild animals being free. Sometimes I share these feelings with others, but most times I keep them secret and I often find myself building pictures of these animals in my mind and thinking about them.

I also like to visit refuges where people look after and protect wild animals such as wolves before they release them into the wild. I admire what these people do to save wild animals from extinction.